# Praise for
## *The Season of Light*

*The Season of Light* is a lovely dance through the many traditions of our varying spiritual journeys. Through these beautiful words and pictures we find a thread that connects us all in and as the Light of the Divine. Enjoy!

> – Rev. Dr. John B. Waterhouse,
> President, Centers for Spiritual Living

*The Season of Light* is an inclusive celebration of the many lights expressed through various spiritual languages and practices. This beautiful experience of light can be a catalyst for discovering and recognizing the universal Light within all creation.

> – Rev. Darlene Strickland,
> Senior Minister, Unity of the Blue Ridge

Beautiful! Wow! Love it! Felt like a blessing just to read it!
> – Cat Finks, L.Ac.,
> Asheville Community Acupuncture

*The Season of Light* projects Love, Caring, Spirituality and Inspiration. It is deep, moving and soulful in the best sense. Nourishment for the mind and the body.
> – Elbjorg Holte Berkenkamp
> Solstice Celebration Workshop Leader,
> Morristown Unitarian Fellowship

# The Season of Light

Open Heart Publishing, LLC
P.O. Box 155
Skyland, North Carolina 28776

Library of Congress Control Number:  2016916558

Collins, Patricia Lynn
*The Season of Light*

978-0-9970613-0-7 Paperback
Printed in the United States
IngramSpark, 14 Ingram Blvd.,
La Vergne, TN 37086
FIRST EDITION

Collins, Patricia Lynn, author.
The season of light / Patricia Lynn Collins.
pages cm
LCCN 2016916558
ISBN 978-0-9970613-0-7

1. Light--Religious aspects--Poetry.  2. Spiritual
life--Poetry.  3. Poetry.    I. Title.

PS3603.O4547S43 2016             811'.6
QBI16-1663

www.openheartpublishing.org

*To the one who shares my life*
*and*
*to the One Who gives me life*
*and the joy of writing!*

# Acknowledgments

I thank anyone who has ever read or listened to anything that I have written. In particular, I am especially grateful to Mr. Vinny Bickler, Mr. F.X. O'Brien and Mrs. Dorothy Sharp, high school teachers of mine who helped launch me as a writer. I am also indebted to my creative writing mentor in college, Marguerite Young, author of *Miss Macintosh, My Darling*.

I am grateful for the love, support and encouragement of my writing by a few close family members and friends: Dr. Carole Kendig, my first and best audience for whatever I write; Mr. and Mrs. Jones, who believed in me when I needed it most; Doug Mendini, who, unbeknownst to me, would "find" and publish my poetry in our college literary magazine; Margaret Henderson, my staunchest supporter; Bernadette Kress; Barbara Barba; Trish McAleavy; Stephanie Soules; Ronna Hermann; Priscilla Hall ("Auntie"); Cindy Bouman; Pamela Henry; Dr. Kristy Fassler; Mary DeLorme; Rev. Chad O'Shea; Aradia Ocean and Carol Smith; Jack Hughes; Andy Werley; Marianne Kilkenny; Deni Niethammer; Lisa Pressley; Sherri B. Free; Mrs. Gloria Howard Free; Marlene and Steve Wechselblatt; Dr. Michael & Margaret Ruiz; Evan Ruiz; Judy Figura; my brother, Daniel Collins; my niece, Tracy Garmon; my sister, Jackie Kobi; and others too numerous to name (you know who you are). I thank you all.

Additionally, I am grateful to Joan Medlicott; Celia Miles; Nancy Dillingham; and Micki Cabaniss. They have been wonderfully supportive and encouraging. I thank you for your kindness and generosity of spirit toward me and my work. And I am indebted to Larry Bruce and Jessi Trimnal for their "Angelic participation" in the creation of this book.

Finally, I am grateful to you, dear reader, for finding your way here to this book, *The Season of Light*.

# Author Notes

I have been writing since I discovered, quite by accident when I was 15, that I loved to write. I had asked a friend to write a poem for me that I turned in as my first "writing assignment" for my high school English class. Much to my dismay, it was entered into a contest and won first prize. I could not let the poem that I had *not* written be published with my name on it, so I shamefacedly confessed my misdeed to my teacher. My "punishment" was to write my own poem about the whole experience. To my surprise, I realized I actually *could* write a poem, and further, that I enjoyed writing it. In fact, discovering my love of writing was a true gift for me; I felt like I had won the lottery!

This marvelous consequence in high school started me on a life-long journey full of words: observations, reflections, processing and sharing my inner-world experience with folks in the outer world through my writing.

My writing journey was not always smooth, however. In my first college short story writing class I almost gave up writing altogether as my professor rejected my work week after week after week, while accepting all of my classmates submissions. I felt dejected and untalented, to say the least. She told me afterwards it was because she actually *liked* my writing style and that my many rewrites were to hone my writing skills. She urged me to continue writing and to publish!

I have had many subsequent writing experiences throughout my life: writing classes; writing groups; public readings. I have written poetry, short-stories, memoirs, articles, interviews and full-length manuscripts. I am grateful for all these opportunities to grow and express as a writer.

My love-affair with words is still going strong.

My prayer is that each of you, my readers, will be blessed by your contact with *The Season of Light*, and that Light will continue to grow in your life. I hope that you will enjoy sharing in these celebrations with me as we embrace together *The Season of Light*. I add my Light to your Light!

-Blessings, *Patricia Lynn Collins*

# Introduction

This story-poem, *The Season of Light*, is an interfaith, multi-cultural exploration of the celebration of Light that is common to many spiritual and religious paths at the same time of the year. This is my recollection of one season's diverse celebrations which I experienced in New Jersey a few years ago. I shared these moments with Dr. Carole Kendig, Rabbi Ariann Weitzman, Mitra Khademi, "Diva" Audrey Davis-Dunning, Elbjorg Berkencamp, Ronna Hermann and Stephanie and Missy Soules. It was a magical time, and I thoroughly enjoyed each one of these activities.

My love of "traveling the world" by way of multi-cultural personal connections was born when I first joined the International Students Association at Seton Hall University back in the 1970s. I was privileged to eat fried bananas that my Cuban friend, Orlando Olivera, prepared for us; to listen to Peruvian love-ballads that Pedro Zavala played for me; to teach Yoshiko Iwahashi how to cut a birthday cake (on our mutual birthday) as she'd not seen one in her native Japan; to help my Chilean friend, Karin Becker, dress for a party; to philosophize about the true meaning of art and life with my Iranian friend, Mitra Khademi; to be gifted with a handmade Chinese village made of cork by the grandfather of Peter K. Wong; and to dance some fancy dance-steps with my Haitian-friend, Jo-Jo Cassis. It was only in retrospect that I realized I was the only American in the group!

As a wholistic health consultant and psychologist, I have had many friends and clients from various cultures, religions and spiritual paths over the years since college. I feel deeply blessed to feel such a close oneness with folks from all over the world, all of whom I consider to be part of my personal human family.

2016

Dear Oprah —

May you fully enjoy my "paper-baby":

# The Season of Light!

Patricia Lynn Collins

And may Light continue to grow in your Life! I add my Light to your Light!

You are one of my personal heroes & you have given me so much! I am happy to give back to you, in my own way with this book!

Many Blessings —

*Patricia Collins*

Open Heart Publishing, LLC
Skyland, North Carolina

I love the peace
and quiet
of the middle
of the night.

Each season
has its own flavor,
its own style
of darkness.

Tonight it is
our Winter Solstice,
when the night
is longest
before the
Light
begins to burn
more fully
once again.

I have honored
tonight's Solstice
with drumming
and dancing,

with chanting
and laughing,
with others
who remain
connected to
our Earth
and the cycles
She goes through.

I have honored
the Great Void,
dark,
but far from empty.
Sitting in the Silence
in the womb
of all creation,

I wait in the
darkness
to hear the
voice
of the One
who guides
my life.

I embrace
the Light
that dances
secretly
at the heart
of all
darkness,

and I rejoice
in the many ways
the Light
is honored
at this
time
of the year:

Solstice,
Kwaanza,
Chanukka,
Christmas;
all are ways
to celebrate
the Light
of Life,

the flame
we dance around,
each in
our own way.

I light
the multicolored
candles
of our menorah,

and I think
of the others
around the world
and down through
time

who
also danced
around the
Yule Log
or bowed their heads
in prayer
as they
lit the candles
in celebration
of the Light.

I go
to the old church,
which has
stained-glass
Angels
that are magnificent
when the sunlight
pours through them
during afternoon
free concerts
through the year.

The Christmas
Service here
is all tradition—
full of
formality and
organ music
and words
handed down
throughout the
years—

the story of
the birth
of Christ,
Light of the World,
Redeemer,
King,
the Son of God,
a gift
to human kind:
Divinity
in human form.

I bow my head
and join in prayer
and lift my voice,
such as it is,
in song,
in celebration
of the
Living Light.

I go
as well
to celebrate
the awakened
consciousness
this season
symbolizes,

not one
God-Son
alone,
but the birth
of the
Christ-Light
in each and
every one
of us.

All part of One,
the Mind of God,
The Creator,
Who has gifted
us with all
creation
and the gift
of creativity
itself

in all its forms
so that we
may
learn to love
ourselves
for who and
what we really
are—
the Light
in form.

I philosophize
about the
Golden Way
with my
dear Buddhist friends,
who seek to walk
the enlightened path,
the eight-fold way,

and to be here,
fully,
right now.

I sing and dance
and clap
in honor of the
Light
in the Kwanzaa
celebration,

delighting in the
music
that streams from
the
giant seashells
played
expertly

as the masked figure
on stilts
enchants,
and somewhat frightens,
the boy scout in
the seat
behind me.

The
multicolored
outfits of the
African dancers
swirl
as they move
enthusiastically,
rhythmically,
magically,

as they dance
to the beat
of the drums,

the beat of
the heart,
the heart light
that burns
brightly
as we join
together
shouting
one final
"Harambee!"

I honor
Great Spirit
while I stand
hand-in-hand
with my beloved
in the Light
of Dawn

as we are
blessed
with sharing
the Eagle
soaring through
the sky,
just for the
two of us,
it seems.

My friend
calls out
to me,
seeking
to understand
her troubled daughter
who,
The Holy One be praised,
seems to have
lost her way
right now.

We discuss
the Qu'ran
and how it
may shed
some Light
for her
on how to
love her daughter
enough
to let her go . . .
for now.

I stop
for a few minutes
to rest
and while
channel-hopping,
find
comfort,
joy,
delight,

in Rabbi Tushkin's
words
that say
goodness
is a virtue
every one
of every faith
may learn to
cultivate,

*so that in living,*
*Light may*
*grow in our*
*experience.*

I am at home
with all the
paths
that honor
Light,
whatever form
the path
may take.

I move from
Solstice dance
to meditation,
from the simple
act
of lighting
my candle

(that's been
blessed by
the Dalai Lama
and by me)
to lighting
our menorah
and
plugging in
our
Christmas tree.

I sing
the Christmas carols
with the choir.

I give thanks for
the qualities of
God:
Love,
Light,
Wisdom,
Beauty,
Power,
Joy,
and
Peace
that are
re-lit
in me.

I walk
in the charmed
circle
of protection
and Love.
Everywhere I go
Love greets me
(as the Light)
for Love
is what I am,

*and you are,*
*too.*

I add my light
to your light
gladly,
thankful to be
sharing Life
and Light
tonight
together

as we celebrate
joyfully
this Season of Light.
I am
grateful
to be here,
once more,
with you.

*The author and publisher gratefully acknowledge the following people for the photographs in this book:*

# About the Author

Patricia Lynn Collins, Ph.D. earned her B.A. in English and Education (1975, Seton Hall University). She holds Master's Degrees in English Literature and Women's Studies (1977, University of Utah) and Counseling Psychology (1992, Seton Hall University). She received her Ph.D. in Counseling Psychology (1999, Seton Hall University).

She is the past-president of Vibrant Life Foundation, Inc., a wholistic health education center, and past-owner of Vibrant Life Whole Foods store. She has lived in New Jersey, Utah, New Hampshire and currently lives in Asheville, North Carolina.

Patricia hails from a family full of abuse, dysfunction and creativity, a common combination. She is a trauma survivor and has counseled many others touched by abuse, addiction and pain. Her family tree is sprinkled with writers, artists, musicians, educators, addicts and psychics. Born into a Catholic family, she has walked many spiritual and religious paths including: metaphysics; Unitarian Universalist; Rosicrucianism; Unity School of Christianity; Church of Religious Science (now Centers for Spiritual Living); Native-American teachings; Earth-based Goddess teachings; Kabbala; Buddhism; Paramahansa Yogananda's and Sanaya's teachings; and she occasionally enjoys Southern Baptist celebrations, as well.

Patricia ends each day writing her Gratitudes and Blessings.

She follows a deep interior "knowing" which she feels is Spirit's Intuition and Grace. Her connection with Angels is profound. She has lived a life full of love, magic and miracles as a result of her deep connection with God.

## Also by Patricia Lynn Collins:

"One-Piece Magic" in *Clothes Lines*. Eds. Celia Miles and Nancy Dillingham. Catawba Pub., 2009.

"The Ant and The Apple" in *Women's Spaces, Women's Places*. Eds. Celia Miles and Nancy Dillingham. Stone Ivy Press, 2011.

"My Mother and Me" in *Drowning Allison and Other Stories*. Grateful Steps, 2012.

"Transforming the Reign of Terror" in *The Cricket and Other Stories*. Grateful Steps, 2014.

"Second Sight" in *It's All Relative: Tales from the Tree*. Eds. Celia Miles and Nancy Dillingham. Stone Ivy Press, 2015.

CPSIA information can be obtained
at www.ICGtesting.com
Printed in the USA
FSOW04n0215041116
26839FS